LOOKING FOR WATER

For Sarah

with Real Joom

Eric Beckr

June 1969

[signature]

Eric Barker

LOOKING FOR WATER

New and Selected Poems

October House Inc. New York

ACKNOWLEDGEMENTS:

Some of these poems have appeared previously in the following publications: *American Scholar, Atlantic Monthly, Harper's, Saturday Review, Harper's Bazaar, Yale Review, Choice, Pacific Spectator, Literary Review, Recurrence, Variegation, Simbolica, Yankee, The Nation,* and *The New York Times.*

Published by October House Inc.
55 West 13th Street, New York

To Harriet Roberts

CONTENTS

I   *FROM* DIRECTIONS IN THE SUN
Listen, The Fog Horns!   11
Spring Dusk, San Francisco   12
The Pigeons and Sun Yat-sen   13
The Pebble   14
The Poet and the Robin   15
Nothing is Always Still   16
Night at Sea   17
Robinson Jeffers   18
Lost Heritage   19
Trees   21
On the Possibility of Unearthly Visitors   22
On a Piece of Driftwood   23
The Pool   24
Atropos   25
Big Sur   26
The Farmer's Dog   27
Poem   28
Birds   29
Isaac Newton   30
My Barefoot Girl   31
Faith in the Earth   32
This, Then, My Heart   33
Night Swim   34
Small Oasis   35
The Country of the Mind   36
Counsel in Solitude   37
In the Wind   38
Sierra Clouds   39

II   *FROM* A RING OF WILLOWS
Spring Song   43
The Green Wave   44

To Yo-Lin   45
Deserted   46
Abandoned Orchard   48
On the Cliff Path   49
Landscape with Figure   50
Little Sur River   52
Whales Going South   53
A Jade Pebble   54
Missile   55
The Rock Pool   56
In Easy Dark   57
A Ring of Willows   58

III   NEW POEMS
For a Dancer on Tour   61
In Thames Ditton   63
I Saw This Sky in England   65
Childhood   66
When She Walks   67
Such Lovely Clouds are Making from the Dead   68
The Rock   69
For Hunger's Sake   70
A Philosopher   71
Drilling for Water   72
A Stone   73
Poem to My Mother   74
And I Will Consider My Cat Caitlin   75
Death of a Poet   76
Poet at Work   77
Under Orion   78
Bird Waking   79
Summer Tourists   80
The Hot Springs, Big Sur   81
A Voice from the Shell   83
A Birthday Poem for Dorcas   84

I

FROM DIRECTIONS IN THE SUN

LISTEN, THE FOG HORNS!

Across their shrouded pastures, through the night,
The bass-voiced bulls are calling one another.
They chew up bales of wet sea-wool like grass
And bawl stupendous love no fog can smother.

But hopeless as it's huge: not one has seen
The Born-In-Sea-Cloud of his giant moan,
Though all night long they roar their loneliness,
Pawing the bitter, ocean-rooted stone.

July's the hardest month of all to bear:
They bellow for their brothers night and day,
But only sea lions tumble at their feet,
Gulls brush them with a wing, but seldom stay.

Lamenting through the Gate, uncomforted,
Like mournful Stentors they invade our town,
Sadder than far-off cannon heard through sleep,
Searching our dreams for solace till we drown.

SPRING DUSK, SAN FRANCISCO

MILKEN as marble through the porticoes
The sea fog draws the twilight in her sails.

Not ringdoves now to dimming woods persuaded
Drop softer syllables through thickening leaves
Than mumbling pigeons huddled on their eaves.

St. Mary's bell adds up a mellow sum
Of seven sonant numbers in the air.

Yellow as daffodils
(as the switch is thrown)
The windows bloom with light round Portsmouth Square.

And up and up the hilly windows stare
And steep and steeper down

Where,

Street by street from the harbor's shrouded water
Evening, seagull-breasted, climbs this town.

THE PIGEONS AND SUN YAT-SEN

CONTENTMENT deep in the throats of pigeons
Bubbled all day like warm spring wells.
Their soft breasts burned like copper shields
Round Sun Yat-sen, their clapping wings
Applauded the weather, the scattered crumbs
Flung from the hands of the generous ones.

"Observe the time and fly from evil"
The text on St. Mary's stones advised.
But only the pigeons flew in sunlight,
Returning to whiten the metal sides
Under the poplars, of Sun Yat-sen,
With folded hands, whose thoughtful eyes
Saw nothing to fly from, nothing of evil
In what St. Francis might have found

(A perch for wings like a full-leafed tree,
Lost in the throbbing and rustling ground)

Better than human sight or sound.

THE PEBBLE

AND LEOPARDS held hot breath the day you flew,
And lions let the springbok leap unharmed.
Sheathing their pointed death, they looked to you—
They had not seen so huge a beast, nor armed
As that tall tower of Gath on Israel's day.
In water green as their nocturnal eyes
When they came down at dusk to drink, you lay—
Tomorrow David comes, Goliath dies.
And in the morning they saw David come
With pouch and sling and take you from the brook
And hold you shining, feel you with his thumb.
And then he smiled, and all the branches shook
In laughter from the hills, the curious sound
That giants make before they strike the ground.

THE POET AND THE ROBIN

(seen together on a garden lawn)

THEIR STANCE breeds silence like a sultry cloud
That all the rain-expectant leaves obey,
A listening attitude enhancing quiet
Like stilted herons in a shallow bay.

Nature provides them with such appetites
That worms will satisfy, or the bronzy sound
Of katydids a branch above the ground.

The cocked heads flow through shadows like a stream.
O they are still as stones. In such a calm
Stood Jericho before the walls rushed down.
A sleeping king from such a garden dream
Was sent to haunt the nights of Elsinore.

The silk of silence straitens to extreme—

A stirring in the grass would set them free,
A red leaf falling from a burning tree.

NOTHING IS ALWAYS STILL

AND STONES can fly like trees
Although they seem so still
In wind they move through waves
That move a standing hill

Whose trees are light as clouds
To float away like weed
As limpet to its rock
Till by waved water freed

With leaves outspread to flow
Through waterstreams like wind
Whose miracle it is
Leaves not a stone behind

But haired with floods of leaves
Makes haystack of a hill
Pours mountains past our eyes
And leaves us standing still.

NIGHT AT SEA

MAGIC is more than it seems,—
Clear weather is the nightwise sign
When the ship's keel
Ploughs the mythology of the sky
And the Dog has a salty bark.

Strike midnight—all is well,
Though the Bull's Eye has a watery gleam,
And Orion hunts with the sharks
The dim and restless Seven.

The world's wheel did not veer
When fire came down in a fennel stalk.
Nor now for whatever port it steers,
Though heaven's hot ore is quenched
Before it falls, and fins
Knife through the stars.

ROBINSON JEFFERS

WHO VALUES a hawk's life more than a man's
Is not without compassion for his kind.
What grows old in the tide's long funeral
And bloodies the enduring stone
Breaks here. If you have picked up
From these wild beaches no single pebble of pity,
Blame your own nature that shrinks
From fathoms where this plummet sounds—
The sea's too deep for it.

LOST HERITAGE

ONCE there was wonder of waking that we shared
With those whose hearts beat simpler than our own.
The birds have not forgotten, nor the beasts,
The afterhush of night upon the leaves,
The stone's cool premonition of the dawn.
They wait beside the light-expectant sea,
They gather by the margins of the lakes;
No doubt is in their eastward-turning eyes,
Always for them the phoenix is reborn.

Then the long miracle of growing day
Grew in our hearts. We held it hour by hour,
The beauty of innocence nothing else could change.

Accepting love, we gave it back to bear
The morning-tasting fruits no frost could kill.
The birds were there before us in the dawn;
The animals with lifted heads were glad,
Knowing their certain god was in the sky.
And we, religious men, traced clues to heaven
In veins of leaves, and in the flowered grass
Read the repeated patterns of the stars.

We were the blessed, the richest heirs of all,
Now poorer than the animals and birds,
Poorer than trees, less eloquent than stones
Of day's long light retreating to the shade;
Of quietness once so germane to our thought
We made a meeting place as lovers do

At evening crossroads privy to the dark,
And love was sudden at the lip and hand,
And close against the heart as quiet as owls.

O now lost traveller, waking in the dark
Night after night to no assuring star.
Remember when the fabric of your faith
With light was sinewed stronger than with steel.
The house you have abandoned is not far,
No farther than the journey that a prayer
Makes to the crannied east, no farther
Than the shadows that the trees

At dusk turn nightward now.

TREES

Most equable of loves
That blow not hot nor cold
Nor whine their claims of loving like the flesh,
But armored in their undemanding bark,
Dig deep, grow tall,
Restore like clouds beyond their own estate,
The cool and temperate climate of the heart.

Days when I cannot reach
Nor listen to their leaves,
Into the mind's full view with wind they come,
Eclipsing leisurely all walking shades,
As prodigal of shadow as the clouds,
But spread in moods more stable on the grass
Of quieter fields than even clouds possess.

ON THE POSSIBILITY OF UNEARTHLY VISITORS

THAT TRUTH might stray into unearthly rumors,
Glintings on strange disk-shapes in the sun,
Landings of friendly strangers come to warn
That our dangerous behavior with the uncaged atom
Imperils stars as precious as our own to their
Inhabitants, is not impossible if we agree
With Hamlet, who was not mad unless the truth be so.
Wherefore sidereal humors may concur,
And walking out one morning after breakfast
We shall be startled out of all familiar dreaming
At what we find imprinted in the snow.

The owl's grave voice implies
That there is more than rain upon the wind.
Some flyers have returned to earth perplexed,
And stories have come down beyond the hawks
Not of a common telling.
There may be signs in heaven we do not see,
And many signs on earth. We might, with profit,
Widen our philosophies, but looking up and far,
Let us not lose that anchorage which made Antaeus strong.
It may be well to listen to the streams,
To gather tidings from the ocean shells,

And plant new groves of myrtle and of rose.

ON A PIECE OF DRIFTWOOD

Ask the sea what kind of wood it is.
Such drenching salt has baffled all I know
Of telling trees by smell. Let the emptying waves,
In their high white confessionals reveal
What this anonymous voyager was named
In blowing wood or field. Look, it has come
So orphaned to my hand of earthly seasons
Not a hollow shell is more imbued
With these sad exequies that dress the
Rocks with weeds. Let the steep waterfalls
Tell up the loud beach how they can change
Earth's liveries to the sea's, and ring by ring
Wash out the long remembrance of a tree.
But in that hush between them let there fall
Some inkling of a rooted heritage,
Of that green name this nameless derelict
Once told through singular fragrance like a flower.

THE POOL

FOR what 's above
Look deep and clearer down:
The images of trees
Grow through the swimming clouds.
Lost in a watery glide
A hawk gives up its purpose in the sun.

Sedate on stilts,
Through sauntering clouds,
A heron minces
And the ripples flow
Continuous with willows where he stalks
Frogs in the waded sky.

Halos become his image:

Doubled in crystal,
Erect in etheric poise,
He steps through widening circles
In the clouds.

ATROPOS

You were the ominous Cloud-Mouth that foretold
With Eden's closing, how all gates would close
On gardens where the trees of pleasure grew.
You were the doom through Joshua's trumpets rolled;
Goliath's ruin waiting in a brook;
Lot's wife's salt-glazing, backward-turning look;
That Christ-forgetting tree Iscariot chose.
You were the sum Ecclesiastes knew,
Who loved Fall's rusting drift, its homing sound,
And the Dark Lover waiting in the ground.

BIG SUR

I LOSE FAITH in words in this country.
Better to leave unsaid
The poems that cannot describe the highest arcs
Of turning and turning hawks, the mountainous
Voyaging leisure of animal-changing clouds.
What words released from this granite shoulder
Can return like a cliff-falling gull
Translating a mood of the sea?
Or strike such wild notes as two hawks now
Down-circling their hazardous air?
Better let the truth be spoken
By what inhabits here from birth:
The autochthonous voice
Interpreting its own environment.
Better to stand and listen
To sounds not alien here.

THE FARMER'S DOG

SPLITTING mosaic of silence like a quake
The farmer's dog who knows no more of me
Than I of him but that outraging throat,
Tears up my fallow field of quietest thought
And barks a nagging bluster through the trees
I grew for shadows and for homing birds.
My roosting doves are scattered in the night
That was a well wherein their muted notes
Fell echoless as dew. The sky was driven
Thick with studs of stars. Their riveters
Had paused, hot hammers held, that silence
From the spaces in between might fall on those
Who thirst. And then that riotous throat,
Scaring the owls of thought within my brain,
Conceiving wordless poems since all words tell
Too loudly what my heart's obsession is,
Although they leech to dove throats in the dark
And listen at the lips of dreamless girls.

POEM

DELIVER ME this crude, amorphous thing,
This knot of bloodied clay to cleanse and knead,
Eject this head of poem like a babe
That I may heal the dark with phosphor eyes
And bell its sullen steeples into song.

Perennial child, born in an austere season,
Hardiest of nature's nurslings in my care
That my green thumb will raise up like a tree
No windy death can topple, and my thoughts
Will roost like birds among its changing leaves.

Beside the sea will come our ending season,
Salt in its veins and fishes at my eyes,
The drowning flood that was our rocking cradle
Mixing its outward drift of leaves and bones
In winter dirges through the ears of shells.

BIRDS

WHEN day's white dancer woke between two hills
The falcons of the morning, swift and strong,
Flashed through the rift with wild and eager cries,
Smiting the silence with a rush of wings,
Drove upward, wheeled, flew level in the light,
Beating the silvered mesas of the dawn.

About meridian's burning hour they'd gone.
On steep and dark, on wide unhastening wing
The vanguard of the sunbright eagles came,
Dropping from aeries on the peaks of flame
Down sapphire slopes of noon.

In heaven's loveliest arc
(Earth's free seem captive now)
From luminous curve to arch,
Dark sails at rest,
From sapphire noon to evening's lupine sea,
They followed down the incandescent track
Curving toward the west,
To shade where shining was,
The matrix of the evening star.

From there the giver of quiet,
Peace bringer to water and to earth,
The shortest-lived before the stroke of dark;
The grey wing-hoverer that must fall and die,
Struck on the wing by night's enormous bird,
Black-breasted with Antares-colored eye.

ISAAC NEWTON

STEMS BREAK, wax melts,—
A thorn of thought worked earthward through his mind.
Apples and gods and mortals all came down
By natural causes or by accident.
Some not unmixed with glory:
That sweet boy, who like a murdered bird,
Fell wingless from the sun.
Rain fell, snow fell.
The magnet at the center of the earth
Drew stars and stones and red-cheeked apples down.
What wonders fell towards that sleepless mole!
What little birds, what great and exiled wings!
Ripeness hung still and heavy from the bough.
He waited for apocalypse to fall,
Feeling the lodestone like another moon
Drawing the earth-shaped apple through the leaves.

MY BAREFOOT GIRL

SEARCHING ALONE through the voices of the sea,
Through rustle and hush like the brittle tongues of leaves
Brimming in autumn drifts as high as her knees,
My barefoot girl goes dancing along the shore,
Kicking up rainbows, stamping up fans of rose,
Shells in her fists, a seaweed wreathed in her hair,
My windrow-raking lightfoot, fallen heir
To the voyaging trove the prodigal waves cast down
For a gull-disturbing infant tanned as brown
As the sand she prints for a time as long as it takes
A wave on webfoot, diamond-spattering heel,
To scatter them sky and shoreward, squawk and squeal.

FAITH IN THE EARTH

FAITH in the earth,
Transmitted through wood and stone
To my feeling hands, the rough enduring symbols
Outlasting human love, the roots deeper,
The fibres tougher, the grave grey heads
Wearing under both skies
Their deep and full acceptance, like the sea.
On the grooved and lichened sides my hand moves,
Spelling like the blind the cycles of dead seasons:
The rages and the calms,
Voices of wind and rain,
The white and summer silences;
In the full-leafed singing shadows
The green love returning under more suns
Than have wakened the oldest of men.

Birds in the leaves do not remember
The full throats brimming round rings
Of old years in their greenshade song.
But my hand remembers—
Tapping through wood and stone
The waters of the aged and ageless springs—
The faith at the fire's center
Burning before birdsong or tree,
The changes in the blood toiling
Through salt streams to the cloud-loved hill;
The tidemarks blind with grass in the growing sun,
And lichen, linked to memories of the sea.

THIS, THEN, MY HEART

THIS, then, my heart
That ticks my time away,
Wearing out years of wonder in my breast,
This tenant, snug within my vulnerable house,
Susceptible to seasons as a tree,
Some winter night will turn the landlord out,
Under a star-deserted sky
On a signless road
Where all the winds' directions are as one,
A naked vagrant careless of the cold,
Poor as he came before that break of day
That ushered in such amplitude of gold,
And showed him, innocent of earth and heaven,
A house to live in, a fire to warm him by,
And for his hunger,
Love's wild-tasting food.

NIGHT SWIM

A HALF MILE out we turned and saw the land
As curious seals must, bobbing sleek heads up,
Carved sheer as cameos in the moon's full pour.
We'd seen them often, like black club-headed kelp,
Remote as floating islands. Bathed in that sea
Of light, they'd seem estranged from us
Farther by myth than distance. We trod water,
Looking back at our familiar element,
The humped and camel-colored dunes
The seals would give a cool appraising stare,
Then slip from sight. Seen from the shore,
What would distinguish us? Against the moon,
Our ball-shaped human heads as black as theirs?
Shrunk in that crucible, identity was broken
On a wheel of light, deceiving sight and sense.
The foam line was division of two worlds;
Illusion held them both, but here the mirage
Flowed and shifted more than on the land.
Our friend walked there, reduced to pygmy size.
He stopped beside the clothes we'd shed,
(Only to enter naked as a fish, these waters
Of the moon, was thinkable) looking out at us,
Then cupped his hands and shouted.
The moon was going down, trawling
A seine of light over the rim of the world.
We waited till the darkness leapt,
Then dived like seals through a forest
Of melting swords as stars like fish
Slipped through our sieves of hands.

SMALL OASIS

MOVE stealthily upon vacant city lots.
Poetry, that random butterfly, is lying
As peacock-eyed (despite the corner sots
Whose bottled week-ends are too long in dying)

As where her fans hover in duskfall skies
An earth-hugged age removed from any town,
Or anywhere her more conspicuous dyes
For good or bad are hunted up and down.

Surprise her in a corner where the grass
Escapes the creeping jaundice, and allays
A sickness bred of gutted tires, and glass
Dribbling the heeltap of the reeling days.

She's even more consoling to the eye
Than if her small oasis were a meadow,
Dearer that westward, by her compass sky,
Her only sunshade is a warehouse shadow.

Oh then give thanks that even here love comes
Bearing no fusty standards on her car
Trailing stale thunder of the deadbeat drums,
But quietly unpretentious as a star.

IN THAT wide country I have named my own
Where none may come unless I give the sign,
The meadow fences are too high for climbing;
No crafty trespasser can pick the subtle locks
Of gates that open at a word from me.

Worn paths lead through the woods, I made them all;
I could follow blind old blazes on the trees.
I cut those deep love notches long ago,
Seeking a path that would lead me to the sea
By sun and moon on the far shores of the mind.

Beautiful is the solitude never once broken
By those whose visitations turn the hours.
I have studied their minds as I study the winds and the tides,
Given them fair skies to the climate of my thoughts,
Our words and our silence are fruit of the selfsame tree.

On a farewell morning by the clock of the tide
It is time to embark again from their port of call.
And I watch them over the sea line crying with gulls,
I hold their dwindling sails in my Gulliver eye,
Homing to their coasts under the creature-changing clouds,
Their fleecy pilots through the weather of my love.

COUNSEL IN SOLITUDE

PRAISE deserts, not hermits;
Mountains, not dwellers in caves;
Not hawks, but the flowing sky;
Solitude itself, not those who inhabit it.
So counsels my heart, telling my days away.
Make room for compassion in your vulnerable house,
But do not praise mortality in the bone.
O pity all the pitiful white bones
In the long funerals of the sea;
The deer and the lion
That die on the mountain side;
The birds that fall from the sky.
But for monuments to praise
Look beyond the grey mirror of your eyes
To those who knew you not
And will not know you soon.
Walk for your words in the shadows
Of mountains, beside the flowing waters,
Under the flowing sky.

IN THE WIND

NOTHING is still—
Not even stones that wear
Such fluent shadows
From the flowing air
Themselves seem not composed
Of anything less volatile than light.
These lucent waves
Set charges to the hills,
Put trees, like clouds, to flight.
Nothing is still—
This landscape like a forest undersea
All wavers from the roots
In wind like water
That unmakes a stone.

SIERRA CLOUDS

STRANGE BEASTS that lose to stranger beasts in heaven,
They come in herds as leisurely as seals,
Browsing among the highest junipers,
Protean as one seen from Elsinore
And maned and multitudinous as waves.
Dawn-emptied of his rage, an old bull mammoth
Leads them up the granite scarps
To last night's streaming battle-seat
Above the jags of falcons and the steep-eyed hawks.
All day they gather round his knees,
Wounded and tired from night war,
Huge-pawed and winged, staring down at us
Like creatures from a lost mythology
Whose ramparts are guarded by griffins
With strange eyes, where peace is deep
And colored like the snow.

II

FROM A RING OF WILLOWS

SPRING SONG

DREAM BACK through driftwood to the nested trees,
Through bird bones to the greenshade song.
All dust is Lazarus, and the dead and gone
Split earth like flowers and bulge the seven seas.

All shrouds are shreds, and waking funerals
Make merry dancers of the walking sighs.
The Lazarus men wink pennies from their eyes,
Unrhyme their epitaphs and plant their holes.

Red over green the mocking blood works through.
Imparted in the narratives of shells
The drowned sing down the sad and wave-rung bells,
The Lazarus sea is washing over you.

THE GREEN WAVE

Now in the Spring, the heaving ground swell breaks
For future flowers, and my heart awakes

And listens to itself below the ground
And knows that darkness by its own dark sound.

The sun grows up, and perfect in their place,
Shine earth and seven seas within its face.

My growing heart, its wild green rage begun,
Lies mirrored in those tableaux of the sun

Where fishes swarm and nesting birds arise;
Lean with the season's hunger in their cries,

The hankering beasts call from the covered wood;
The green wave drowns the fasting in their blood,

Turns mine to sap and rises in the tree,
Roars in the earth, is quietest in the sea.

TO YO-LIN

(Asleep on the morning of her twelfth birthday)

THIS morning
While you were still sleeping
I made the toast
And brewed the jasmine tea
And brought them to you on a tray.
But you were not yet awake
And looked so far away
From all things waking
That I would not disturb you.
Your rooster has crowed from the hen coop.
The sun has climbed Pico Blanco,
Driving the fog in a golden hood, back to the sea.
When you wake
I shall be working in the lower garden.
Call out to me from the open window
And I will bring you twelve ripe strawberries
One for each year,
And two white lilies:
One for the table
And one for your hair.

DESERTED

EVERYTHING in the house was like the kitchen door
The wind blew halfway open, waiting
For wind to blow it shut again.
Everything in the house was like that:
Half-open or shut; falling asleep
Or sleeping; everything in the garden
Either dying or dead. But when the wind sprang up
That hollow shell was full of sound
As a conch is of the sea;
The rotting curtains and the dusty webs
Swaying in the same wave
As the dead flowers in the garden.

I came upon it first on such a day
And stopped to look in through a broken window,
And the wind rushed in behind me,
Scouring it like a bell,
And poured out through the other side
Flattening the wild oats in the opposite field
With its broad and whistling scythe.

And I went on, not caring for that sound,
Though I love the wind as well as any man
Close-lived to woods and fields,
And often lie awake at night
Simply to listen when it walks the roof
Or lets me know it's in the chimney
Or stroking the backs of the nearby sleeping birds.

But that wind had a different sound.
I cannot tell you how it filled the house
Unless you've wondered how Niobe mourned.
It made me think of those who lived there once,
Who must have chosen such a cloud-loved hill
For what to them was seeming permanence.
And what ill circumstance had tripped them up,
And set against the walls those smouldering fires
That eat a house to death with shameless wounds.

ABANDONED ORCHARD

THROUGH fruitless years
The pocked and dying trees
Gather green memories
Like old men in the sun—
Barrenness back to plenty;
Skies that were mists
Of their own blooming;
Apples grown red in the cheeks;
Heavy and swollen in the pause of time
Ripeness hung golden
As the last of leaves
Lovelier for dying, brightest before they fall.
Bereft of bird song, at the end of shade,
They keep their old directions in the sun,
Feeling through naked twigs to buds and leaves,
Tapping green rivers through remembering veins,
Hugging the warmth of past meridians
For comfort in their cold and winter age.

ON THE CLIFF PATH

I LOOKED down over your shoulder at the sea.
Alarm in the grass presaged the coming hawk.
The shadow fled you darkly as it fell,
Now even the stones are gentle.

So nearby night shall dark intentions show
And deepen by their nearness, what I love.
Be threatened in my arms. Love, so enhanced,
Makes danger beautiful,

And rests you safer where you rest your head,
Being more secure for being what you are.
Then, hazards, fall, all armed and harmlessly,
Leaving you more beloved.

An oak tree in a hilly pasture
Had been his calendar for twenty years.
For twenty Springs he watched the leaves come out,
As many Autumns saw them fade and fall
And earth take all.

Before the cold set in, with axe and saw
He cleared the dead and left the green to thrive.
(It was an ancient tree before he came,
Giving a little back each year to earth
Until he built close by his house, and hearth
That grew in Winter such a hungry flame.)

Warm days in Summer on the grassy heave
Fitting his back like water he would lie,
And look through leaves and lichen at the sky,
And wonder whether wind or worm would bring
Some dying limb to fall—,
'Sometimes they hang for years. Perhaps
My hearth will grow cold first, and the slow sun
Waste without warmth my winter fuel away.'

It was a thought that did not fret his mind.
One way or other would be well for him
Whose love of sun and grass was long and deep,
And living close to earth, lived close to sleep
Safe in the circle of the earth's quiet wheel.
The overtaken tired on pad and wing

From his high acre every year brought down,
He witnessed, and his mind accepted,
Though in his heart, as at the fall of leaves,
There stirred the sharp and annual lance of pain.

And when the dry twigs crackled into flame,
Chafing his calloused hands before a blaze
That burned upon the ash of winter days
The west wind had made bountiful for him,
He read without much sadness in the fire
His own unheralded and small defeat
On some cold Autumn's end of wind and rain:
The dead wood heaped for burning on the hill,
The grey dead hearth, the house untenanted,
Absorbed in death, the oak tree dark and still.

LITTLE SUR RIVER

I HAVE followed Little Sur to the foot of Pico Blanco,
Under cottonwoods and alders, under the green tents
Of the redwoods where smoky sunlight lies tangled
In bramble and fern, listening to white laughter
In stony places, to the green soliloquies of pools.

Between the intermittent green and silver
Leaves of willows leaves of alders
I have heard her singing in a shroud
When so many grey ghosts come up from the sea
Anonymity thickens, identity is lost;
No tree or flower in the sea's white shade
Is surely named for love.

When Pico Blanco wears sunset like a lion skin
On his granite shoulders
I have followed her down to the sea
Where gulls and cormorants burn like phoenixes,
The great ocean is possessed by light and sound.

Now for two years the river has been my pilgrim neighbor;
Many ties are broken, many loved voices lost.
Human affections grow deeper than any bond
In nature, she cannot fill their absence.
Yet here, beyond the malaise of the time,
Is a voice unfailing for the heart's acceptance,
Counsel better than the words of sages,
Than philosophies that fail
In the face of the ruinous fact.

WHALES GOING SOUTH

(seen from the Big Sur Coast)

LIKE HILLTOPS turning in a cooler green
As if all earthly springs had lacked the rain
To make up for one always submarine,
Wet bash of flukes, drenched echo in the brain;

For one half-wheel of shoulder half immersed
Not growing flowers now nor any weed
But remnants of Sargassos when they burst
On matted sea lines curving as they feed.

Humping those arcs, to follow and to flail
Out memories of dry seasons when they stood
Anchored in hill rows, victims of the fail-
ing waves' estrangement to their seas of blood;

To loss of mile-down deeps and rimless tides
In tropic driftings cooled by their own showers,
Dreamed Tritonward when meadows of their sides
Lay earth-becalmed in seas of grass and flowers!

And now relaunched to plow the hill-change deep,
Led by their bulls in endless moonward runs,
Cruising their seaworn cirque, awake, asleep,
Bulging horizons like a school of suns.

A JADE PEBBLE

THROUGH a piece of jade
Given me by one who felt the sea
Move its deep moods
Through rivers of her blood,
I have unlocked a narrative of tides
That told away a face of sea-green stone
And left such cradled news as shells impart
In rounded pebbles fitted to the thumb.

Like salty rumors winding through a shell
The texture of this stone reminds me now
How closer than all countries lies the sea,
No farther than its nearest messenger.
Inland among sand and desert trees
Hear how it swims upon the wind
And with that overtaking fills the air
Till gulls cry down the hawks,
And islanded, I stand and rock
To movements of the sea.

MISSILE

WATER had smoothed and shaped it for such work
As would promote a shepherd to a king,
Bring down a living mountain like a bird,
For it was changed when fitted to a sling.

And what had given it purpose was the stream,
Wearing it with the long perpetual wave
That is time's operation, and will bring,
By that sure motion, each man to his grave;

Whether he comes to glitter huge and tall,
A loud defiant target in the sun,
Or from his purling arsenal rejects
All flawed for flight, and keeps the deadly one.

THE ROCK POOL

WHAT have you brought back from that clear and sea-
    rinsed day
Beside the unblurred vision to the far horizon;
A pelican's catapult ripping the bright water skin;
Arnold at Dover and every beach to say
Live true and deep, time shortens every summer?

Yet at a chance encounter why should I wonder at all,
Knowing your mind but little, your heart even less—
But there was a pool of coral and glistening pearl
Brimmed by the tide, asleep in timelessness,

And deep enough for a group of sirens singing
There lost time back across that famous sea—
The pelican struck close by as the hot sun dried us,
Flat as the slap of an oar in the Odyssey.

What have you brought back from that clear and sea-
    rinsed day?
For me the tide of memory flows so deep
Day cannot follow where blind fathoms drown
All but what brightens through remembering sleep.

IN EASY DARK

I GO by touching where I have to go,
Obedient to my own illumined hand.
I part the darkness, and I follow slow.

In easy dark I feel how light can grow.
The night is what my fingers understand.
I go by touching where I have to go.

What tells the wind and where the waters flow
And plots direction that my eyes demand?
I part the darkness, and I follow slow.

A travelling world is what my hand must know,
A sail by water and a staff by land.
I go by touching where I have to go.

My hand is eyes' sure distance: to foreknow
The reef of shipwreck, the engulfing sand.
I part the darkness, and I follow slow.

Nor guttering wind nor wave can overthrow
This light that lights the rock on which I stand.
I go by touching where I have to go.
I part the darkness, and I follow slow.

A RING OF WILLOWS

for Jean Kellogg

THIS shallow pool holds such a depth of sky
That all our sorrows are taken pity upon
Where any angel, weeping his steep bright tears,
Compels a look for heavenly compassion
Down from an upward searching of the clouds
To where the sky is doubled, and the trees,
In perfect likeness of their looking down,
Look up from heaven that the pool conceives.

They all are willows, flowing in a ring
Deep dark and down, a green and thickset fall
Towards heaven nearer than the birds ascend.
Framed in that water-wish, their mood is all
One downward concentration like a crane.
He stands on one slim stilt, himself absorbed
In proving stillness by his still intent,
Balanced upon a white and windless cloud.

III

NEW POEMS

FOR A DANCER ON TOUR

for Madelynne

I KNOW a dancer; when she moves among
Sad, ancient cantos, then I walk along
Ravenna's evening river, and I hear
Paolo to Francesca, lip to ear.
She keeps a feeling for the lovely old
And makes it live within a living mold.

I saw her dancing on the village green
At Stratford (or I saw she should have been)
On Shakespeare's birthday, for none seemed to know
How quick those dead had gone on heel and toe,
Or how to smoothly make and break a ring—
I went away to hear the blackbirds sing

Not more of April than its greatest day
That gave us Will of Stratford. A field away,
An English field! I saw her coming down
That hill which climbs the nearest to the town.
Through flowers in pride of blooming down she came
With all the blackbirds whistling for her name.

I saw her once at Venice, in the Square,
With pigeons on her shoulders and her hair;
A pecking bird was perched on either hand;
Among applauding wings I saw her stand,
A sister to St. Francis; now I go,
Thanking my lucky eyes that this was so.

Let her choose cities for that time of year
Which favors them, and so enhances her.
Let her select what's natural as her own,
That place the gods let fall their incense on.
Something has gathered there, perfect in time,
Matching a season matchless in its prime.

IN THAMES DITTON

In Thames Ditton I remembered a clock
Drawn on the bottom of my father's straw hat,
The hands pointing to three o'clock.
This is how you tell the time, he said.
But in those quick years I cared no more for time
Than a gadding May fly or a climbing lark
Unless it told me when to seek a field
Whose single beech tree by its inching shade
Showed me how time was measured by the sun.

In Thames Ditton I remembered a sign
Rhymed and creaking in the wind
Inviting thirst inside The Harrow.
Time had circled forty years
The clocks of fading dandelions
When I went back and found it there.
There it hung and nothing changed.
And I stood there, remembering words
Blown across a summer field
Of dandelions died out of glory.

A wider whispering evening now
Filled the branches of the beech.
A thicker shadow on the grass
Travelled towards the end of day.
I leaned with love against the tree
And looked across the golden field,
The prime before the dandelions
Begin to show their greying clocks
For wind to blow the time away.

And this is how you tell the time,
Moving quietly overhead,
The evening wind was telling now.
Deep and dark across the field
The shadow of the beech tree fell,
Birds were settling in the leaves,
And soon the field would nod asleep.
This is how you tell the time,
A grave away, my father said.

I SAW THIS SKY IN ENGLAND

I saw this sky in England. Looking up
Between two trees I saw those creatures there.
That other field was pushing at my back,
Spring was over England everywhere.

Birds rained it down. Cows dribbled where they lay
More buttercups than grass. I think I slept,
Or half asleep from hum and dazzle, fell
Into a dream that I have always kept

To happen where it will. For clouds don't change
Unless you want them to, but come to dwell
In that long mood that holds them in their place,
Still as a fern's reflection in a well.

Youth leads them into age. O I was young
When I resolved those happy gods as mine.
Their blowing cheeks blew such a song to me
That love came radiant, water changed to wine;

The minutes paused to show their miracles
So slowly turned that tall field round.
A lark sang in the highest tower of cloud—
I listen, fastened to the falling ground.

CHILDHOOD

In those days I took all things for granted,
Gifts for the simple reason of being born.
My longest scruples ended in a sigh;
The innocent indifference of the dawn

Made me cruel as a knife, but never guilty.
I observed the natural laws of Life and Death.
Apt at my games, I stalked the lowly,
Small kingdoms withered in my fiery breath.

Close on my wake of funerals, came a girl.
"Discover me among the nodding grass," she said,
"And find the natural balance of those laws
You follow blindly without heart or head."

I made another death. But while we slept,
That virgin rose and touched us tenderly.
"It was a green and easy grave," she said,
"Remember me with love and rosemary."

And changed the ignorant aspect of my eye,
Indifferent as the innocence of the dawn,
To look with growing wonder on the why
And lovely wherefore of my being born.

WHEN SHE WALKS

for Germaine

I KNOW a lightfoot woman
Who, when she walks,
Lends to what she's passing
Her most natural way
Of gladness in her going
As if to say
"Nothing is really still.
Look how the trees
Come towards me dancing
And are left behind,
Conducting their own music
In the wind;
Bird and petal and leaf
Are on the tide
That flows the fields along
On either side;
And what is then
More liquid than the stones
In wind that blows such lightness
Through my bones?
Earth turns, and in her turning,
Giddies me, until I stop
And stop the nearest tree."

SUCH LOVELY CLOUDS ARE MAKING
FROM THE DEAD

A POEM can cast a cool shade overhead
To lie between your forehead and the sun.
Such lovely clouds are making from the dead.

Great Andrew Marvell was the one I read
To Margery that summer afternoon.
His poems can cast a cool shade overhead.

A nearby brook was telling where it led
To that salt mouth where all loose waters run.
Such lovely clouds were making from the dead.

A maiden may give up her maidenhead
When shadows bless the ground they rest upon.
A poem can cast that good shade overhead.

"That poet knew how love is made," she said,
"He makes me want to lie with nothing on."
Such lovely clouds were making from the dead.

We gathered ferns and made a marriage bed
And Margery took her clothes off, one by one.
A poem can cast a still shade overhead,
And lovely clouds are making from the dead.

THE ROCK

for Jean Burden

THIS branch-rocked morning
Under the yellow farewell showers
I walked down to the river
And crossed the wooden bridge.
Now I sit under the alders,
Looking at the rock. Littered
With autumn leaves, the river flows;
Wind empties the trees in gusts and swirls
And fractures in the pool below the rock
Reflections of the swimming clouds.
Yesterday you were there, looking deep down
To your clear hoist in space,
A mingling of descent and altitude
Equated by the water's level,
Where trees grow through the clouds
And most real fish inhabit
An insubstantial heaven of the birds.
Now the rock is empty. But the wind dies,
The glass of memory to its still depth returns,
And you come back in that second sky
Where trees and stones resume
Their clear, untroubled places.

FOR hunger's sake,
A hollow bag
That winters in its skin;
For hankering in the veins,
The green years fallen thin;
I steal the crumbs of birds,
Unspring the loaded traps;
Count back the phases
Of the lovers' moon
To when she swam,
Abundance to her rim,
Through my full nights.

But memory
Is a wanderer without home:
The tracks are blind with grass,
The landmarks gone;
The moon, my lantern
Through the lovers' shades.
The last one led
Along a late way home,
She dogs me down
Towards that common dark.
The world is shining
In another's hand.

A PHILOSOPHER

THOUGH they took the trees away
And locked him in his room,
Nothing could break that green allegiance!
When I went to see him
He was sitting very quiet, looking
At his painting. It was called "The Wood."
But even one tree had given him shade enough
To hide the naked walls and wind enough
To blow the ceiling off!

"They're with me all the time," he said,
"Just thinking on the one
Has brought the whole grove in."

DRILLING FOR WATER

DOWN BELOW the cat's-claws we know there is water.
It has been proved time and again in this land
Where charity above ground is the rarest miracle.
So we drill towards China,
Bringing up sand and rotten granite
On this first day of the Joshua-blooming sun.

(But those trees the Mormons named
Don't reach with roots,
But grow from bulbs that swell like pumped balloons
Storing therein those liquid cool reserves
That make these desert-beckoning trees in April now
Thickset with creamy blooms among their thorns.)

For water is the kindest element.
Even far underground that virtue shows
Long before it is seen
Or climbs for us to listen to.
As now in contemplation of the end in sight,
The shining snake controlled
Whose coils contain the very truth of dreams,
We hear it singing merrily in the pipes,
Watch its prodigal rainbows in the garden to come.

Sweating under a sky that has always too much blue
We drill between the cat's-claws
Bringing up sand and rotten granite.
But the hawk's high cry is
Water   water   water
The Joshuas open and the lizards sing.

A STONE

It goes down deep and dark, a sort of lump
Of deity to kneel to in its way
Of never interrupting what you say.

What sways your world? A Cloud-Mouth in the sky?
A woman crying with the voice of Eve?
It must be that in which you most believe.

It must be something that you see or hear:
A wind among the trees, a steady fire
That will not die unless the heart expire.

A trunk, a pillar lifting what you praise
Above the clouds, or what the clouds dispose.
It must be that which faith can never lose.

What moves the mountain moves the smallest stone.
What I have chosen is not very high,
Half underground and half against the sky;

No fallen star with lightning in its veins
Still lurking hot for leaping in the grass,
It makes no plea for notice as I pass

Into the radius of a moving quiet
That draws me earthward on a compass hill
Within a circle that is never still.

POEM TO MY MOTHER

MY MOTHER fell from such warm days
Their fragrance would not leave her hair.
That summer longing all her life
Mocked out the cold funereal air
And opened all the windows wide;
My mother could not rest beside
A river without wandering there.
She was that midsummer bride
Fallen from so full a rose
To the measure of a sparrow;
In the bed she looked so small,
Frail beyond all belief,
A wind might move her as a leaf,
Ah, the little shape she made!
Downcast only as a ball
To bounce back in Fortune's face
When that reckless bitch would turn
Her wheel for blind and senseless harm,
She leaves tomorrows all bereft
Of celebrations early birds
Will miss for scattered crumbs,
(Her plump melodious thrush will find her gone)
And canticles whose every praise
Was tenderness, before this darkness
Stopped her dead, her singing way to sun.

AND I WILL CONSIDER MY CAT CAITLIN

TWANGED through Cat Heaven the utmost toughest thread
Of nine car-dodging lives but never snapped.
Eight knocked out, the last one nearly dead,
She limped bloodily home from the grave's edge of the road.
You, so easily suggesting the mercy shot,
Consider my cat Caitlin clean as a swan shift,
Lying in her own ordure, the long dirty agony of the ditch.
And I will praise Christopher Smart, and the vet,
Setting her broken jaw and one leg, as I listen now
To the terrible sound of her unsheathed claws
On the window ledge, through my lulled house
The frightful miaow's beware to the mousey wainscot
Of eight lives risen from the dead.

DEATH OF A POET

WHEN the feeding springs became dry mouths,
Alders lost their reflections;
The river bed cracked like a map
And he went away, following his own directions.
Plotted out in his last poem, they are
Taking him everywhere and nowhere, anonymous
As a leaf in the wind. But here,
Where he disappeared in the dwindling mirrors
And his voice petered out among the stones,
He comes back clearly in his favorite season,
On this first day of the returning clouds
Under the blowing alders, in the remembering stream.

POET AT WORK

WHAT holds him to his groove
Is what he feels the words will say
When he unlocks their meaning:
Fertility of wombs! A girl could rise
And thank him for the glory
Of her breathing; a beast
Could spring; a single bird
With that one song
That's always worth the hearing
Lift up his head in sheer mad glad surprise!
They're there for every damned and lovely thing
He loves for growing through his mood. Whatever:
Woman, tree, bird, beast, stone, flower,
Will keep his head down till their language tells
Without equivocation what they are
And gives his poem their special voice for speaking.

SOMETHING far out had touched me in the night
And called me up to think about the time.
From where I lay, through the showery darkness
Of the equinox, I could see the patchy clouds
Unveil and blot the moon. Perhaps
If I went out and looked straight up
I'd catch a flying glimpse of him at least.
That he was back I knew, and lying overhead.
What had reached out might well have been his sword.

The rain had stopped, and shaking cloud rack
From him as he walked, went that great man.
(To me he always seemed more friendly than the others,
Like those on earth that throw the longest shade.)
I watched him till another shower moved in,
Then left him in the summer-ending sky
And went to bed and listened to the rain.
My watch said 4:15, but I'd been told:
A roof can keep out weather, not the time.

BIRD WAKING

FEELING the tree
Turning under me,
I wake in a straight line
Towards the sun,
Knowing exactly
Where he will break cover
And touch me with his warmth.
High in the leaves
(attuned to my pitch and balance)
The morning
Swells in my throat—
The joy of praise upon waking!
Up here
(knowing what I can do)
I sing before I fly—
In the eye of a hawk perhaps,
A rash devotion—
But what are hazards
That hover the air
To this pure waking?
Such love all risks attend,
Morning after morning.

SUMMER TOURISTS

THE signatures
Of their untidy lives
Litter the beaches, foul the rocks.
Here in Big Sur, we must wait
Late autumn's high cliff-reaching surf
To annul the dirtiness of human behavior.
Then overnight the sea will work like fire;
In the morning the immaculate sand
Will receive the prints of killdeers and gulls,
Impressions natural and beautiful
As the patterns of shells.
Then we can walk clean, for a whole season
Nothing is defiled. We can even forget,
On that first sea-drenched morning,
What stale infections fed the sun's increase,
The long, slack degradation of the tides.
Meanwhile, think of that green rage,
That scouring water,
Think what fire is.

THE HOT SPRINGS, BIG SUR

(in the Roman tub)

THROUGH these hot throats,
A gull's short flight
Above the kelp-dark sea,
I breathe an air that breeds
A tropic mind, become a sensuous
Slave to touch and smell;
Immersed in warmth,
Luxurious to the chin,
Give indolent answers
To the curious gulls
Shrilling cold sea-news
Through my hothouse air.
O Molly and Mary, you are far away!
Why should I think of you now
In your tiled bathrooms,
Turning the gleaming faucets,
Admiring your rosy flesh
In mirrors while you bathe?
I can hear the wild trumpets
Of the whales, and sometimes catch
(Before it disappears) a black
Half-wheel of shoulder turning south!
Should I persuade your way an envious eye?
A Roman senator, I loll
And lave, drawing from these
Benevolent natural springs
Elixir for the tiredness
In my bones, draining

The day's long sweat and ache away
Through these kind throats
That sing me half asleep
A cormorant's cry
Above the dark weed-swollen sea.
O Mary and Molly, you are far away!

A VOICE FROM THE SHELL

WEDGED between rocks, a clutch of eons,
I cannot escape the dead. Their dying
Invades me with cries, rumors of wreck,
News coming from so far a distance
It is an unknown place, empty of all but
Loss. An island perhaps, whose loneliness
Is the worst of deaths, or water
Everywhere and always crying
Kill kill kill kill kill
To swell my drone of elegies. Clutched
In a vise of time, I am haunted by the
Drowned. Their funerals fill me with
Tales even for the yet unborn, whose
Mothers listen to my hoarded news
And tell it in their sleep.

Since, being a dancer,
She makes move
Whatever lies beneath her;
Nothing is stable where she goes;
A tall field yields
As easily as to wind
To that cool motion in her;
May her birthday
In this month of fallen streams
Hover the needle
Between west and south
And rouse that weathercock
To which our rivers rise
And lost reflections gleam,—
So we may walk this day
Between two clouds,
Bringing her rosemary
And the last of leaves,
Remembrances to grace her head,
Where, taught by birds,
She teaches in the air,
Her feet unlock the stations
Of the stones, and rivers
All run with her.